Colin Jones & Poems of Note

D1146928

PPD@LCC
London College of Communication
Elephant and Castle,
London SE1 6SB

Colin Jones & Poems of Note

COLIN JONES
and poems of note

Editor Tony Wailey

Colin Jones & Poems of Note

Published by iKraal
P.O. Box 5326
Kenilworth, 7745
South Africa

First Published 2006

Text copyright © London College of Communication 2006
Images copyright © Colin Jones 2006
Editor: Tony Wailey

ISBN: 0-9585088-1-X

Designed and Published by iKraal, Cape Town
Printed and bound by KKS Printing, London

Colin Jones & Poems of Note

Foreword

Colin Jones is a photographer who is now in his late 60s. He was the original Billy Elliot, a working class youngster who joined the Royal Ballet in the early 1950s. As he travelled internationally as a dancer he started to take photographs and later joined the Observer in 1962, working with the likes of Michael Peto and Bill Brandt. It was a continuation of his journey after he had finished with the dance.

This book features 30 of Colin's images, some of which were published by Phaidon Press in 2002. Entitled "Grafters" they are photographs mostly centred on working class communities of the 1960s - the world of the steelworks, the mine and the shipyard where a tight frame sketched a community together and contrasted with the paradoxical and contradictory world of the waterfront with its intense localism and far horizons. Other images reflect the tension between home and flight, community and self, rootedness and metropolitan glitz. All project an experience that is still being validated today. Together they form a continuum of the artists' development and a relationship with the students that the college still enjoys.

What should also be said is that Colin's dyslexia remains defining and critical in the relationship of text to image. He has been a great enthusiast for the idea that students from all Schools might write to his images. This is Widening Participation in action where difference proves no barrier to progression and which we like to think we do rather well in terms of professional development at this College.

Colin Jones & Poems of Note

PPD (Personal and Professional Development) and Creative Writing students from across the different Schools of the London College of Communication have supplied poems and prose fragments as text to these images. What makes this publication a particularly exciting development is that students have had the opportunity to work with established creative professionals. To be engaged in publications such as these provides a great opportunity for involvement not only as enthusiasts but also as professional practitioners, whatever the field, within the creative communications industry.

This aspect of personal and professional development is something we encourage, in conjunction with academic rigour, across all of our undergraduate programmes. It gives me great pleasure to provide the foreword to this publication and to have our students' work recognised alongside an artist whom the Sunday Times has characterised as the George Orwell of British Photography.

Dr Will Bridge
Head of College, LCC
University of the Arts, London

Colin Jones & Poems of Note

PPD at the LCC

The great teacher of the New York based "Method" School; the brash and brassy Stella Adler once told Marlon Brando that the most successful professionals, actors, designers, artists, and managers of communication networks, always worked from multiple perspectives. It is this that the author, Jack Mezirow, calls transformative learning. It is from such an outlook that we try to structure Personal and Professional Development at the London College of Communication.

Personal and Professional Development is how we look at the world through different eyes. The central theme from PPD that we hope to leave you with is the concept of reflection and more importantly its counterpart, critical reflection. Reflection about yourself, about where you have been, where you are now and where you are going is all-important in constructing a framework of professional development in the creative industries.

Critical reflection will enable you to determine how best to arrive at your destination and supply you with multiple perspectives along the way. This includes exposure to other bodies of work, habits, creative constructions, feelings, cognition through texts and images which will help assist you construct a critical evaluation of how you develop yourself. You will take PPD as a credited unit across each year of the undergraduate curriculum. Each year the emphasis will change slightly in accordance with your own chosen discipline as you develop your own interpretative and critical faculties. Personal and Professional Development has become a significant strand of the University's provision of your curriculum.

PPD in your first year will consist of the development or consolidation of academic standards, of self diagnosis, evaluation of cultural artefacts, formal styles of writing, reports and essays: in short, the technical development that you will need to succeed in an institution given over to the Media, Design and Communications industries. The forthcoming year of academic study will include the keeping of a reflective or professional Diary. This will help you record and document your own learning processes: something of importance across all professional fields. This is as appropriate for those going on work experience as for those engaged in simulated work projects and includes your own individual reflections on the learning process and the ways in which you learn best.

Critically reflective essays in your first year help you enlarge this very personal process into a critical summary, where you will draw upon the work of other authors in order to construct a framework based upon your own learning processes. This will also be achieved via presentations, report writing or in the production of other academic essays, which have your discipline at their core. An illustration is given below.

Technical (Year One)

LEVEL 1

- Diagnostic Assessment
- Learner Development
- Presentation Techniques
- Group Work + Reports
- Time Management Concepts
- Academic + Formal Writing Skills

In the classical academies of music, categories of artistic merit are placed upon those who achieve "a deep interpretative capacity" of the Masters' great works.

In your second year of study, PPD will help you move towards preparing

Colin Jones & Poems of Note

for projects in your particular field: interpretations of others' work is the critical theme of this year, again however your learning is the central character to the plot. This may be through the consolidation of work based learning for Foundation Degree students, or gained through intermediate and integral projects for Undergraduate Degree students.

Extending your critical summary which builds upon your reflective diary PPD will now ask you to prepare a Career Path Analysis, which again is based upon your own experiences and skills, but asks you to place them within a more objective and critical framework appropriate to your particular professional field. At the end of the second year you should be considering yourself as a relatively autonomous professional and focusing accordingly within the different strands of your own discipline. A professional Curriculum Vitae accompanies this analysis.

For Foundation Degree learners the end of the second year is the time when you effectively leave the college and continue your work in industry. All students however have an opportunity to be considered for transfer to the 3rd year of an honours degree programme providing their profile is of sufficient standard and they complete a bridging course which is linked to the PPD programme. In taking PPD in years one and two, context, skill and personal development become huge influences to the linkages of a critical framework for such FDA students wishing to continue.

If the interpretation of your own professional role is critical in year two, then a combined programme of outside specialist speakers, all practising professionals, adds to and complements the further development of your interpretative capacities. Again the intention is that this will enable you to critically reflect upon your own performance at a particularly crucial point in your studies. The Enterprise Centre, the Creative Careers Service and the Cross College Elective programme all interact with PPD at this particular moment of your academic career, to assist you in forming multiple perspectives of both yourself and your particular industry.

Colin Jones & Poems of Note

Interpretative (Year 2)

LEVEL 2

- Concepts of Team Work
- Work Placements
- Work Related Learning
- Employability + Careers
- Enterprise Initiatives
- CVs + Career Path Analysis
- Bridging Programmes

The recent head of the BBC's World Service suggested that the secret of arts management lay in the value of having a good story to tell, to have others who work with you, believe in it and who are then able to tell the story themselves. These are the articles of the PPD.

In his book the Seven Habits of Highly Effective People, Stephen Covey (1994 ed) asks us to consider the role of time management in a professional life not as a series of notes or jotters or "to do" lists, but as a series of conceptualisations as considered as much by Hawkins in the field of quantum physics as those by Hollis in Graphic Design.

Time management is crucial to Graduates at the end of their 3rd year of study in that they should be looking at PPD not only as a way of understanding and demonstrating the research methods of their own major projects, but also the personal research objectives within their own professional field: to consider themselves as research objects and to diagnose what is still needed in their own development. An engagement with the process of project management both personal and professional is vital here.

Colin Jones & Poems of Note

A dissertation proposal and intermediate progress report form the major part of the PPD programme for this year. In terms of professional development, Exit Dossiers provide the link between intellectual characteristics of the discipline as well as professional advice, tips, networking and the updating of professional CVs for future employment possibilities. In this way PPD hopes to encourage reflection and critical reflection, not only through our students' specialist disciplines, but more importantly through themselves.

Critical (Year 3)

LEVEL 3

- Research Methods
- Research Proposal Planning
- Progress Report on Self Management
- Dissertation Management
- Speakers + Futures Programmes
- Self as Research Object: Exit Strategy Dossier

Exhibitive

This publication, assisted and developed by working professionals and as a book of images, initially published by Phaidon in 2002, is the work of the photographer Colin Jones in collaboration with PPD students . In 2004 the work formed the basis of a major exhibition entitled, "Text to Image" that was held in the college throughout the Spring of 2004. The contributors to this programme were year 2 and 3 PPD students combined with those who were taking "2nd year Cross College Electives" in creative writing, another feature linked to PPD.

Colin Jones & Poems of Note

Further exhibitions have taken place. PPD students within the Schools of Graphic Design and Media have collaborated with the Design Writers Group "26", in being engaged with a project that has featured at the London Design Festival in 2005.

More of these exhibitions are planned across all of our Schools in which students engage with professionals in order to enhance artwork, visual media or text within the field of communications. This is an enhancement of the reflective and critically reflective categories promoted by PPD in the first two years of study at the college.

This professional liaison also enhances the separate cognate disciplines that feature at the College. Colin Jones was so delighted with the work of students for his exhibition that he donated all of the exhibited photographs to the college as part of its permanent collection.

We are looking for similarly great things from our recent students as well as those joining us in the near future. We hope through the PPD programme to encourage you to become a divergent and transformative learner and to take for granted the ability to bring multiple perspectives to any particular situation that may arise within your academic and professional life.

References

Covey, S., (1994 ed) *The Seven Habits of Highly Effective People*, New York: Simon & Schuster.
Mezirow, J. (1990) *Fostering Reflection in Adulthood*, Oxford: Jossey Bass.
Moon, J. (1999) *Reflection in Learning and Professional Development*, London: Kogan Page.
Moon, J. (2002 ed) *Learning Journals*, London: Kogan Page.

Tony Wailey,
Director of H.E.Development
London College of Communication

Colin Jones & Poems of Note

Contents

Colin Jones & Poems of Note

Colin Jones & Poems of Note

Colin Jones & Poems of Note

Mission

Is this where you dreamed your great dream
With clouds and ships blowing down the Scotty,
Docks and cranes and new condominiums
Stretching away to the Northern Sea
Can you see my square from your hotel
The cantilever bridge, the spirit warehouse
The hexagon clock of Jesse Hartley
the yellow sun on the window bars
or is your crystal light, blind
To where I am standing
behind the spangle, back to the clock house
Back to the tobacco dock, read forsaken
by ships and singers, smokers in alleys
Steel mills with slates out, facing the stages
The emigrants coming down slow
Taking it in turns to eat, sleep and blow
Their silences into other worlds
Battered bags to catch the stars
Throwing rages at other sons,
How many lives can one person live?

Anon
PPD & Creative Writing

Colin Jones & Poems of Note

A street off Scotswood Road
Benwell, Newcastle-upon-Tyne, 1963

Four girls dance playfully
on a street of earth
and upturned cobblestones.
Behind,
a brick wall of proletarian houses,
an array of enticing posters,
displaying products of the times.
Stark contrast between
reality and glamour.

Joyce Saunders-Diop
BA Digital Media Production 3
Personal and Professional Development
School of Printing and Publishing

Colin Jones & Poems of Note

Children playing in front of a corner shop (Detail)
Benwell, Newcastle-upon-Tyne, 1963

Take them to a far place
where they can see the sun
and smell the fresh air

see the world and all its
Beauty
show them that the rundown
streets of Tyneside
are not the ends of life

they are only the roots of a
beautiful large oak tree
and once we break through
this pit of soil
we can see what lies above

Kanda Faraj
FDA Design for Graphic Communication 2
Creative Writing Elective
School of Graphic Design

Colin Jones & Poems of Note

Children playing in front of a corner shop
Benwell, Newcastle-upon-Tyne, 1963

The duck's dove
What you put in that gravy?
Now listen carefully

The recipe
Two teaspoons of sugar
3 apples
2 carrots and a bit of flour

Mix good and bake for 30 minutes

Maria Karpouchina
BA Graphics and Media Design 2
Personal and Professional Development
School of Graphic Design

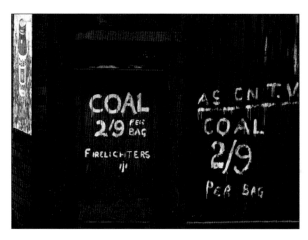

Coal merchant's shop (Detail)
Benwell, Newcastle-upon-Tyne, 1963

sometimes I feel I could also turn blue
I will burst
if her voice continues to ring my ears
My legs are feeling numb
pins and needles running up the soles of my feet
I sway slightly
Exhausted
My eyes roll backwards
Uninterested
I only intended to nip out
for five minutes
Pick up some fuel
hoping not to bump into
the biggest gossip in town

Tulin Malecki
FDA Graphic Design 2
Creative Writing Elective
School of Graphic Design

Colin Jones & Poems of Note

Coal merchant's shop
Benwell, Newcastle-upon-Tyne, 1963

I'm back on the edge again
struck like the lines
On this sunlit railway.
illuminated by labour
I walk unchallenged, miles from home
with the Jungle coming on.

Tony Wailey
PPD & Creative Writing

DAD

When you hit the road
I was seven
Does it make you proud

You missed me grow
You wouldn't know
I'll reflect on this in years to come
I'm a man now; it's too late
I did all this without you around
Does it make you proud

Matt Ringsell
FDA Digital Media Production 2
Personal and Professional Development
School of Printing and Publishing

Railway Line
Newcastle-upon-Tyne, 1963

Who is he? I don't like him. He's not from our street. He looks funny and he tells us to pull faces at him. He looks like a monster, not a visitor, dressed all strange. He doesn't look comfy here. I don't like him. His friend keeps sniffing like he doesn't like the smell of our street. Richard is worried. He has stopped playing. Standing still makes me colder. Why is he here? Why is he writing things, making us look like little dollies? I squish my face up so he can't take any more pictures, but he seems to like this even more. 'Perfect, she's really framing it, 'Today' is going to love it!' Richard begins to cry.

Nicola Carey
BA Book Arts 2
Personal and Professional Development
School of Printing and Publishing

Colin Jones & Poems of Note

Children in the Street (Detail)
Peterlee, County Durham, 1964

The day after the night before
Brother and sister stand together
Children lost and alone
The boy clutches a small toy guitar
Looks up to the camera
Unsure and confused
You can still see
The remains of the inferno
Through the girls' eyes
Soot, black soot
It's out now.

Kim Viner
BA Marketing and Advertising 2
Creative Writing Elective
The Marketing School

Colin Jones & Poems of Note

Children in the Street.
Peterlee, County Durham, 1964

What does this man think of eternal salvation?
I can only make assumptions
But the eyes reveal
the state of the heart and the soul of men.

Ben Bell
BA Book Arts 2
Personal and Professional Development
School of Printing and Publishing

His life reflected on the lines on his face
Sadness transmitted through his eyes
Lost in the crowd of darkness
As if life is passing him by
Everything seems empty
He doesn't know which way to turn

Lucia Rodrigues
BA Marketing and Advertising 2
Creative Writing Elective
The Marketing School

Coal miner
Seven Sisters Colliery, Dulais Valley
South Wales, 1997

Expression without meaning
Shows on his face
No glimpse of hope
No faith in his eyes

Katja Fausch
BA Marketing and Advertising 2
Creative Writing Elective
The Marketing School

I want to walk on roads
that don't fill my leather
shoes with the dirty
sewer waters of
the valley

Kanda Faraj
FDA Design for Graphic Communication 2
Creative Writing Elective
School of Graphic Design

Coal miner
Onllwyn Mine, Dulais Valley
South Wales, 1985

I see the drunks tumble out all fists and cuffs. Years ago I'd have stepped in. Not no more. Best to keep your head down, notice no-one, hope no-one notices you. Not that Its hard for me. I'm known 'round here as the quiet and moody type. It's not true, it's just easier to let them think that way. I'm the lone wolf me. I spot a bit of skirt shrieking back from the fight expanding in front of her. Wouldn't mind a bit of that I think, but too much bleedin' effort, isn't it?

Nicola Carey
BA Book Arts 2
Personal and Professional Development
School of Printing and Publishing

Colin Jones & Poems of Note

Coal miner (Detail)
Dulais Valley, South Wales, 1985

Working for what seems like years
in the blistering heat
Cold he no longer feels
Hoping he reaches the end
and banish the anguish of many years

Julia Markou
BA Marketing and Advertising 2
Creative Writing Elective
The Marketing School

Colin Jones & Poems of Note

Coal miner
Dulais Valley, South Wales, 1985

Old, old as the hills
and strangely near
take a break
roll a snout
grab some snap
sit back
where are the kids?
I'm too old for this.

Graham Crew
FDA Digital Media Production 2
Personal and Professional Development
School of Printing and Publishing

Sunday dinner at night
A few pints by the black water
Then a bunk up
Freshen the blood before walking
The pit on Monday morning

Tony Wailey
PPD & Creative Writing

Coal miner after shift
Seven Sisters Colliery, Dulais Valley
South Wales, 1997

41

I wash off the filth accrued from a hard, long, filthy day
bubbles of water and soap roll down my body
yet to reach my dark, black face
this rag, torn and tatty, like the body it is washing
filthy, scraggy hair, worn-out, overused
dirt on my face

silent animosity within this miner
as in all miners
a humane picture to an inhumane reality

Dan Simpson
Foundation Media
Personal and Professional Development
School of Media

Colin Jones & Poems of Note

Coal miner showering after shift (Detail)
Rhondda Valley, South Wales 1987

Finished work. Showering
who the hell's that looking?
tattoos stuck like bolts
to the end of his camera
Will he have the pints,
the club, the music, the nights
to know what else is coming?

Charlene James
BA Marketing and Advertising 2
Personal and Professional Development
The Marketing School

Coal miner showering after shift
Rhondda Valley, South Wales 1987

When the rural meets the industrial or
when the industrial grows onto nature:
houses, metallic structures and electricity poles
Cut across undulating slopes of earth
On which ponies are grazing
with their sharp vertical lines

Joyce Saunders-Diop
BA Digital Media Production 3
Personal and Professional Development
School of Printing and Publishing

Exhaustion
the land – the people – the pit – the ponies
Wasted and dirty

Wheels spin in the wind
and wires whistle

Sally Spencer-Davies
BA Digital Media Production 3
Personal and Professional Development
School of Printing and Publishing

Colin Jones & Poems of Note

Seven Sisters Colliery
Dulais Valley, South Wales, 1965

a black silhouette
a woman with a pram
she heads for the light
walks down an empty, dead road
a tunnel with no exit, no escape
claustrophobic
symbolic of the society she lives in
everything is dark and industrial
factory roof, gas works and electricity pylons
she heads for where the sky has opened up
and cast a ray of light
the light 'at the end of the tunnel'
where she picks up her husband's wages

Dan Simpson
Foundation Media
Personal and Professional Development
School of Media

Colin Jones & Poems of Note

A coal miner's wife picks up his wages
Sunderland, 1963

In Argentina the angels sing
about love and death
On flowers in the morning
waiting by the water
dependent on our keeping
a hold of the balance
between mine and floor
and the archway of the social

Kelly Erez
BA Marketing and Advertising 2
Personal and Professional Development
The Marketing School

Colin Jones & Poems of Note

Mining village (Detail)
Washington, County Durham, 1963

Seeing her slowly
Set out for evening Mass
Beneath the moon in winter
The geese above
Black heels, trim as steel
Honking beneath the stars
The kids home
Their moans at night
Two wives ago
I walked these marshes.

Sometimes we think we know
and rationalise the dross to
understand, the way it runs.
To have it all, this third life.
To laugh with women.
In love, with food and sun
But in winter to hear the Geese
fading, the kids calling
Next to the sea, the salt marsh
In silver and moonlit frost
You do get to thinking
in the lee of her cross.

Tony Wailey
PPD & Creative Writing

Mining village
Washington, County Durham, 1963

Colin Jones & Poems of Note

Giants

advancing up through a sea of metal —
appearing through a mist
of despair and fixed fixture.
Hard edges
cut the sky and
offer no mercy.

Sally Spencer-Davies
BA Digital Media Production 3
Personal and Professional Development
School of Printing and Publishing

Colin Jones & Poems of Note

Walking to work at Swan Hunter's shipyard (Detail)
Wallsend, Newcastle-upon-Tyne, 1963

A feeling of movement being interrupted
Not just spectator but participant
Awareness of land shaped by man

A border between
Urbanization and industrialization
Strictly correlated
Industrialization brings urbanization

Time standing still
Landscape of desolation

Leonardo Lopassio
FDA Digital Media Production 2
Personal and Professional Development
School of Printing and Publishing

Colin Jones & Poems of Note

Walking to work at Swan Hunter's shipyard
Wallsend, Newcastle-upon-Tyne, 1963

Skeletons of intellect towering above the horizon.
Will the dream be awoken to overshadow the dirt of the
gray skies?
Patching the dirt of the earth with layers of brick
washes the dream away.
Yet,
The progress proceeds above their heads.

Maria Karpouchina
BA Graphics and Media Design 2
Personal and Professional Development
School of Graphic Design

Anxiously waiting
for the whistle to blow

Shantelle Carty
HND Retail Management
Creative Writing Elective
The Marketing School

Shipbuilders waiting for the end of their shift (Detail)
Dundee, 1979

10.20: The captain of the Bytom, Mr. Catnose was called onto the bridge. Three minutes later he had finished his cigarette, passed through half his 420 metre tanker and stood next to the second mate glancing directly onto the shore.

10.38: The radio screamed " Here, La Coruña harbour, steer your vehicle as far east as possible!" A decision has been made.

10.42: The workers on the scaffolds on the northside of the area sensed an abnormality and started waving their arms. First at an arriving ship, then at their colleagues further up the shore.

10.46: A 200,000 ton steel giant slid up the beach east La Coruña. The recently assembled buildings crumbled under its weight; the workers ran; Captain Catnose prayed.

Nils Porrman
BA Graphics and Media Design 2
Personal and Professional Development
School of Graphic Design

Shipbuilders waiting for the end of their shift
Dundee, 1979

Wm. Higgins:
Your brown stool and corner
Your wings beat again
like the great phoenix.
across the sun,
your spirit beats on.

Jason O'Harro
FDA Digital Media Production 2
Personal and Professional Development
School of Printing and Publishing

She needs a new coat – I need the work
How long has it been
The new fellas go bare headed – bare faced.

Live to work – work to live.
It's what he's always known.

Sally Spencer-Davies
BA Digital Media Production 3
Personal and Professional Development
School of Printing and Publishing

Dockers collecting for a colleague unable to work
Liverpool, 1963

This is a picture of the times, a historic portrait that reflects on the 'waiting' and community culture of Liverpool Dockers of 1963. The Dockers wear uniforms - hats, trench coats, dark trousers, shoes and shirts. They huddle together, like penguins - smoking, talking and waiting for work on a street corner. They look old before their time. Everything around them is dark and gloomy, mirroring their moods. The picture provokes notions of the depression in Britain and America in the 1930s.

Dan Simpson
Foundation Media
Personal and Professional Development
School of Media

Colin Jones & Poems of Note

'The Lump' - dockers waiting for work (Detail)
Liverpool, 1963

Standing together
but each for their own.
Coats flap in the wind
like the black wings of the crow.

Faces beneath caps
grow hard;
Thoughts hardened into habits
in the years of waiting.

Sally Spencer-Davies
BA Digital Media Production 3
Personal and Professional Development
School of Printing and Publishing

Colin Jones & Poems of Note

'The Lump' - dockers waiting for work
Liverpool, 1963

I've got 3 kids and a fourth on the way. We haven't had any meat
of proper food for two weeks. I hate having to fight with my friends
for work, but in 1963 in Liverpool, it was the docks on the dole. My
Catherine shouldn't be shamed like that. Dear Jesus - please pick me.
Please let me have decent work. Desperation mixed with anticipation -
everyday the same. We had a boy - John, two weeks early, but a fighter.

Alison Coxworth
BA Retail Management 2
Creative Writing Elective
The Marketing School

Colin Jones & Poems of Note

Docker (Detail)
Liverpool, 1963

Solemn face, laughing eyes
Stares past the camera deep in thought
Thought about something meaningful
Thought about another place
      away from the docks
    the dirt
    the noise

A quiet place a peaceful place
A place which gives a solemn face
Eyes that can laugh

Kim Viner
BA Marketing and Advertising 2
Creative Writing Elective
The Marketing School

Colin Jones & Poems of Note

Docker
Liverpool, 1963

I don't have much
My world engulfs me
I am exultant

Gary Brosnan
FDA Digital Media Production 2
Personal and Professional Development
School of Printing and Publishing

Colin Jones & Poems of Note

Woman in curlers at '77 Sunset Strip' boarding house (Detail)
Blackpool, 1966

She sits in yellow and drinks aghast,
She swigs down wine to face the past,
The men, the noise, the ships that blew,
She's known them all, the worthless few.

The river hears her sigh and croon,
Of stolen nights and sunlit days,
Berths and piers in golden haze
The lovely men she knew.

Like September on the Dingle,
With her Sunday parlour song,
By repair shops and half tide locks,
There's no fun remaining single.

This Blackpool bar of smoke and dreams
That always leads you to the sea
And on the Sunday afternoons
Waves like corn in a Bacardi breeze

And a dream is more a dream
In the yellow light of Spring
She's on her feet, the Jukebox screams,
Men start rocking when she hits,
'Joelene'

Tony Wailey
PPD & Creative Writing

Woman in curlers at '77 Sunset Strip' boarding house
Blackpool, 1966

soaking up as much sun
before it disappears
for another year

Matt Ringsell
FDA Digital Media Production 2
Personal and Professional Development
School of Printing and Publishing

Drifting in and out of sun-drenched sleep
the washing swaying and flapping like the sea.
Is there a future
beyond a galvanised bucket?

Sally Spencer-Davies
BA Digital Media Production 3
Personal and Professional Development
School of Printing and Publishing

Colin Jones & Poems of Note

Waitress sunbathing (Detail)
Blackpool, 1966

Colin Jones & Poems of Note

My hair blows with the slightest
summer breeze
no noise
no words
Just the leaves the trees and I
We have become one

Kanda Faraj
FDA Design for Graphic Communication 2
Creative Writing Elective
School of Graphic Design

Waitress sunbathing
Blackpool, 1966

The first thing I ask
what is she thinking
Looking bored
mundane life of serving tea
and smoking cigarettes
All day

She looks slightly concerned
one of those trances
A million miles away

The composition is good
definite fore
middle
and background

white nicely balanced
with the notices
The pinny
and the
Tea

Matt Ringsell
FDA Digital Media Production 2
Personal and Professional Development
School of Printing and Publishing

Waitress at '77 Sunset Strip' boarding house (Detail)
Blackpool, 1966

Colin Jones & Poems of Note

A velvety lass
Spring on her apron
Irene Gilpin's best uniform
Grimethorpe or Cawthorne
It makes no difference.

Heather Symonds
PPD & Creative Writing

Waitress at '77 Sunset Strip' boarding house
Blackpool, 1966

'Nymguh' she mumbles, her gob wrapped round her ice-cream sandwich.
She's trying to talk to me. I pretend I can't hear. Stall some time til I
have to feign interest in her dull, moronic conversation. In this aspect,
I'm glad she stuffs her face, it keeps her quiet, makes it easier for me to
hold back the flesh clinging irritation every time she opens her mouth.
In exchange for the quiet, its toll, is the wobbling mass of pale, dimpled
skin and broken, veiny thighs that climb into bed beside me every night.

Nicola Carey
BA Book Arts 2
Personal and Professional Development
School of Printing and Publishing

Colin Jones & Poems of Note

On the seafront (Detail)
Blackpool, 1966

Colin Jones & Poems of Note

One two three
how to get it right
how to stay clean
and enjoy the cream.

One sit up right
two hold it never tight
three lick the middle
before you work the sides.

One two three
How to get it right
How to stay clean
and enjoy
the ice cream.

Maria Karpouchina
BA Graphics and Media Design 2
Personal and Professional Development
School of Graphic Design

On the seafront
Blackpool, 1966

You had five kids
You wrung out blankets by hand
You made great stews
And pies.
You did the crosswords and once transposed
Notes into another key
On the piano at the Hotel Gresham
In Dublin
They said it was Rose Heilbron
But it was you who got their ARCM.
At aged twelve
You deserve to win
At Bingo.

Heather Symonds
PPD & Creative Writing

Playing Bingo (Detail)
Easington Colliery, County Durham, 1999

Bingo, hairnets, not on your life
big rings, part timers, wives
Older now, hands, raffle tickets
vinegar, chip butties,
six carder management
Big women, big appetites
a glass of wine

Dawn Mansell
BA Marketing and Advertising 2
Personal and Professional Development
The Marketing School

Playing Bingo
Easington Colliery, County Durham, 1999

I feel slightly nervous as she speaks to me, even though in my opinion she isn't necessarily worthy of all the accolades she receives. I find myself leaning forward slightly to make myself heard, her crinkly eyes smiling, her goose neck craning. After a few minutes I realise she's not really hearing what I'm saying, just nodding in the appropriate spaces. I ponder idly how wild my language could get before her balding brows would raise in shock. She too, appears to be wearing footwear much akin to the ballet shoes I am wearing. Funny, mine are designed to aid rapid movement, hers to provide the comfort to merely shuffle onwards.

Nicola Carey
BA Book Arts 2
Personal and Professional Development
School of Printing and Publishing

Colin Jones & Poems of Note

Royal Ballet School rehearsal (Detail)
London, 1962

She wasn't French at all and her overacted vernacular sounded stupid, but I didn't dare to tell the old lady. Funny what an iron grip one's education has on one's tongue. The whole situation was idle and smelt mouldy. She usually dressed ready for a sudden stroke or heart attack, though the second seemed unlikely for her garlic breath. We were accompanied by an old record player that jumped and scratched whenever the trains passed nearby. Then the single large mirror would shiver and put our second selves in a funny flickering. I guess she made up our marks by the amount of time one could stare into her false teeth grinning. I was fed up with it, others never got tired.

Nils Porrman
BA Graphics and Media Design 2
Personal and Professional Development
School of Graphic Design

Royal Ballet School rehearsal
London, 1962

Colin Jones & Poems of Note

Rough plaster pink ridges
Welded over strong piggies
Soon to float as strawberries
One cream gauze
On a Pavlova tune
No scarlet ribbons for this.
Ailing bird, Bravo, Encore.

Heather Symonds
PPD & Creative Writing

Prima Ballerina - beautiful and precise
She rises on her points above the pain
Beneath the make-up
Her skin, coarse and tired
Her feet bleed and harden

Sally Spencer-Davies
BA Digital Media Production 3
Personal and Professional Development
School of Printing and Publishing

Colin Jones & Poems of Note

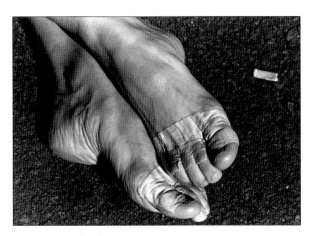

English National Ballet, dancer's feet
Sydney, 1999

Why, Why Why?
perfume and cheap wine.
This girl looks fine
Stay a bit longer can't you
food on paper plates
will she leave him
turn turn
our audience gone.
Anymore to drink
Anyone to love
Some party this.
I think I'll have another
one.

Samuel Afework
FDA Digital Media Production 2
Personal and Professional Development
School of Printing and Publishing

Colin Jones & Poems of Note

Royal Ballet last night party on stage at the Royal Opera House (Detail)
London, 1961

legs crossed arms lying by my side
as still as the air around me
humid the day has become
all the creases of my body perspire
holding back all sudden movement
a tense aching
on the border of fantasy

my surroundings I have absorbed
I feel free
the smell of nature enters my lungs
as I inhale
my head is light with every breath
I exhale

Kanda Faraj
FDA Design for Graphic Communication 2
Creative Writing Elective
School of Graphic Design

Royal Ballet last night party on stage at the Royal Opera House
London, 1961

take a deep breath and don't let your wits get the best of you as you
pass what is known as hemisphere an experience that will make you
feel the same weight as the ant clouds become two they are split by
the hands of mother nature's most devastating creation as high as the
sky and powerful as the sun dominating vast green lands and towns the
white cream top makes children gaze with hunger to climb high peaks
and take a bite for me on the other hand it's a bite of death

let me breathe and exhale away from being enclosed greatness was upon
me energy of another kind took my soul away it's a clever trick to be
harmonious until I breathe fire and turn the white cream into lava

Jason Kennedy
FDA Design for Graphic Communication 2
Creative Writing Elective
School of Graphic Design

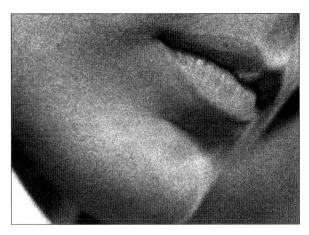

Royal Ballet dancer in her dressing room (Detail)
Glasgow, 1962

I am tense
yet I want the feeling
to stay
it's a good tense
if I keep going
I will find
what
I'm looking for

Kanda Faraj
FDA Design for Graphic Communication 2
Creative Writing Elective
School of Graphic Design

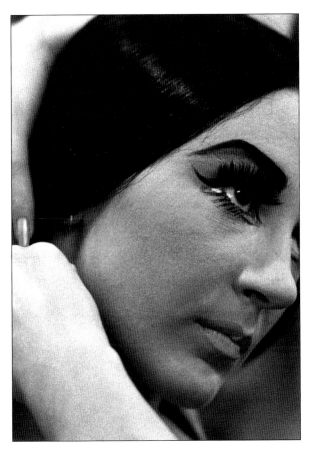

Royal Ballet dancer in her dressing room
Glasgow, 1962

Rivers will flow into oceans creating waterfalls
Strangers we will no longer be
Fly without wings
Even catch you when you fall
As we converse in harmony

Lynette Dias
BA Marketing and Advertising 2
Personal and Professional Development
The Marketing School

Colin Jones & Poems of Note

Break during Royal Ballet rehearsal (Detail)
Sunderland, 1961

the one with the cowardly long face mistaken for a horse yes that's me
with my long stick arms sweaty palms using my knees as a towel only
to leave an imprint of my right hand shaking with fright to show my
moulded sour face I dread the humiliation that shatters like raindrops
and pierce my skin with a thousand emotional needles pouring poison
throughout my body

all I have is sweat locked in a heated box thrown away in a corner never
meant to be open or unchained

butterflies couldn't tell whether they should stay or leave my bones
rattled as though I was a rattle snake a rattle held by a baby

Jason Kennedy
FDA Design for Graphic Communication 2
Creative Writing Elective
School of Graphic Design

**Break during Royal Ballet rehearsal
Sunderland, 1961**

I believe the importance of existence is to exist,
When you move, move as though
You have more life than a butterfly,
I suggest that you feel, before you see.

M. Tamer
Foundation Media
Personal and Professional Development
School of Media

I bent down
my legs intertwined with one another
my left arm stretched into the air
pushed with every stance
Drummed
beaten with words
It will happen
if I keep trying

Sau Phan Tu
FDA Design for Graphic Communication 2
Creative Writing Elective
School of Graphic Design

Northern Ballet Theatre dancer
Halifax, 1991

time has lost its meaning
I could stay in this space
forever my chest moves
with the motion of the trees
the branches are my nerves
reaching through the breeze
the air kisses my skin as it
gently flows by dodging
all the rivers to reach me
and my space
my eyes
open wide
from the chill
that has arrived

Kanda Faraj
FDA Design for Graphic Communication 2
Creative Writing Elective
School of Graphic Design

Colin Jones & Poems of Note

The Gorbals, Glasgow (Detail)
This image appeared in the Independent Review
30th November 2003

'Their ship came back from the Mediterranean like a prize fighter, crossed the bay unmarked and continued north along the west coast to Glasgow. Discharging oranges and wine on the bag of a big wind, salt all over her. Glasgow, a town like Liverpool full of dreams and madness. The banging, shouting shipyards, the lashed waters of the Clyde, winter coming down like shrapnel from big guns. Joey and himself drinking in bars and clubs along Plantation Quay. "Communism is more than just a nice idea pal" says Joey after twenty wines.'

Tony Wailey
PPD & Creative Writing
American Women
Northern Lights, 2002

The Gorbals, Glasgow
This image appeared in the Independent Review
30th November 2003

Colin Jones & Poems of Note

Professional Development and Simulated Work Based learning

Our students need to work with professionals in every field of the creative industries if the attendant results are projects, publications and exhibitions that encourage and publicise student endeavour to produce such work as in this excellent collection.

A well-designed and resourced work-based or professional liaison learning experience can provide a wide range of learning opportunities, which enable the student to relate their college-based learning to the world of work. It can enable the student to develop specialist technical skills and knowledge, understand the importance of work-related disciplines of time management and working to quality standards, note the importance of meeting deadlines, good communication and interpersonal skills.

Most importantly professional learning works with a perspective that allows students to see themselves as designate professionals and to work within a correspondingly professional light. This quality alone can enable the student to develop increased self-confidence and self-esteem, such as that shown by those students who have worked on the production of this present publication.

There is little doubt that the concept of Work Based Learning, which is provided through a work placement, can bring special value not only to the Foundation Degree but to all of our Honours Degree programmes as well. It is clear that this concept of learning through work experience is central to the model of vocational higher education, as envisaged in the development of the Foundation Degree. At the College however, we hope to go beyond the strict alignment of this concept and are trying to realise it as a general design principle for professional development for all our degree programmes.

In certain occupational sectors, travel and tourism, hotel management and catering, nursing and motor engineering, work-placement is a well-established aspect of education and training. However, in other areas of creative production, reductions in the work-force numbers and consonant pressures have meant that fewer and fewer companies have the capacity to offer work-placement. This is often simply down to having insufficient staff capacity to accommodate and manage a placement student. Increasingly stringent regulation in the workplace has also brought further restrictions on what can and can't be accommodated within the working environment, especially where potentially hazardous processes are involved.

Increasingly sophisticated, computer managed production environments where most of our graduates embark upon their careers can also create restrictions for placement students wishing to gain access to work experience, particularly within the communications, media and design industries. In some situations, the demands of production, and the cost of expensive 'down-time' when errors are made, mean that the placement experience provides little more than a 'standing by Nelly' observation and no chance of actual 'hand-on' experience. Therefore one of the key problems with work-based learning in the workplace is that availability is limited only to those sectors of employment where it is the norm and can be accommodated and effectively managed.

The Printing and Publishing sector, for example, is characterised by the 80-20 rule, with 80% of the sector being comprised of Small and Medium Enterprises with less than 20 employees. The sector is also subject to very harsh operating pressures, with high levels of investment in increasingly automated and lean manufacturing systems. This has created an environment where the capacity to provide placement, even in medium sized operations, has been severely restricted. In Surface Design and Digital Media, the sector is again characterised by SMEs with many companies comprising only a small team, with freelance services being bought in on a project-by-project managed basis.

Colin Jones & Poems of Note

In these fields, course teams across the college decided that work-based learning could only be provided as a college based simulation. Working with professionals who attend the college is therefore vital. Fortunately our Schools have the production facilities to enable such teams to devise work-based learning experiences that are designed to closely simulate the kind of experience that a student might gain on an industry placement. Professionals coming to the college and working with students on these projects enhance this process. It involves utilizing both the human and physical production resources at our disposal, increasingly the case across the College in Graphic Design, The Marketing School, The School of Media as well as in the School of Printing and Publishing.

In this way a series of models for development, related specifically to work begins to emerge. The projects provide for:

- Student design and production teams, establishing roles and responsibilities (communication and negotiation)
- Industry client briefing (communication, analysis of requirements, clarification of brief)
- Design and production team meetings (confirming/negotiating roles/responsibilities/leadership, planning, organising, meeting, communicating, setting and meeting deadlines, reflecting on team and individual performance)
- Client progress meeting - presenting and agreeing design solutions (communication, clarification, negotiation)
- Production (allocation of tasks, setting deadlines, completing production to agreed standards and deadlines)
- Product presentation, evaluation/client feedback
- Group-based and individual reflection, peer and self-assessment.

Within such projects academic staff, technical staff and outside professionals are able to fully contribute to the student experience. The industry-based client plays an important role in bringing an external and professional focus to the experience. This is important since the external client establishes the standards set for the work that is required and provides valuable feedback from the world of creative business and industry.

Other models of simulation have been adopted within our Schools. In each of them the course teams have sought to provide opportunities for students to apply theory in practice and to develop the work-related skills of planning tasks, organising work plans, scheduling work, taking responsibility for a set of tasks, carrying out tasks to specified standards of quality and to the setting and agreement of deadlines. Most of the models involve both individual and group based working. All involve the development of transferable skills in communication, planning, negotiation, organisation, reflection and peer and self-evaluation, qualities that are sought by potential employers in the creative industries. In this way the college supplements the role traditionally taken by the work placement student.

These models could not exist without professional input. A recent example would be the exhibition of work by students in the Schools of Media and Graphic Design in collaboration with the design writers group "26". Work produced included posters and videos exhibited at the London Design Festival, this work was then collated into a professional publication and sponsored by London Underground. Here resides a golden opportunity for our students' work to be shown and published in very quick succession.

In circumstances where the availability of good quality work-placement is limited, and there is the likelihood of considerable variability in the quality of experience that is available within the particular industry sector, then work related learning as simulation is a very practical way of focusing learning via coursework into the skills needed for work. This is also why the Personal and Professional Development Scheme is vital for our students.

Colin Jones & Poems of Note

One of the most valuable aspects of simulation is that it is a designed experience in which standards of learning can be applied and the outcomes measured, but most importantly in the series of liaisons it produces with practising professionals, who do most to influence and boost our students outside of the everyday academic demands of their chosen degree. Simulated work-based, or work-related learning and professional development is here to stay and builds upon and extends the historical traditions established by this college in the fields of Art, Design and Communication.

Professor John Stephens
Dean of Printing and Publishing 1995 - 2005
London College of Communication
University of the Arts London

Colin Jones & Poems of Note

Career Path Analysis - Examples of PPD Assignments

When reflecting on one's self and one's individual development Covey's Seven Habit model can help in directing and establishing where one is at, where one is going wrong, and where a better future lies. In reflective learning people can establish and answer many questions of themselves. With the exception of the last point the model reflects that of how a business may also run itself, through reflective individuals and their attempts to move forwards. Whilst an enterprise may look at its current position, problems and how to change them effectively, in attempting to analyse yourself and your own position, this model can be extremely useful in a personal context.

Covey's Seven Habits
Personal attitude, a private victory
1. Be Proactive
   Be aware of yourself, your strengths, weaknesses, blind spots, motivations – and be proactive in finding out as much as you can about yourself.

2. Begin with the end in mind
   In summary, create and live by a personal mission statement. This may lead onto more specific goals and objectives, but the idea is that you try to live as the sort of person you'd like to be remembered for when you've passed on.

3. Put first things first
   Define what it is that really matters in your life, then spend your time on those things. Rather than spreading our time thinly across too many activities, concentrate on doing a few things well.

Environmental interaction, a public victory

4. Think and win

   Be aware of yourself, your strengths, weaknesses, blind spots, motivations – and be proactive in finding out as much as you can about yourself. Then be proactive in applying that knowledge to your relations with others.

5. Seek to first understand then to be understood

   Put another way, "God gave us two ears and one mouth, and they should be used in that proportion." In your communications, be sure you know the other person's point of view before you start expounding your own ideas.

6. Synergize

   Look for ways to take your ideas and other people's ideas and build on them together, on the basis that the outcome will be something greater than the sum of the inputs.

7. Sharpening the saw

   Renewing yourself – Physically, mentally, spiritually and emotionally.

Figure 1: Adapted from Coveys Seven Habits (Chimaera, 1999)

Current Analysis.

At present the career goal is University where the aim is to achieve and exceed with the chosen subject. Obtaining a degree with honours was always a career goal within my educational path. The path through education was a simple one and of linear form. Unlike many other colleagues the path towards obtaining a degree was without disruption and pauses.

In choosing which subjects to work with to obtain this goal, the options were taken relatively easily. It has always been apparent from peers that students should pick what they feel they enjoy and will find easy to excel in. This has been present at all times, through GCSE, A-level, AVCE and degree selection.

At times it has been questioned whether the chosen subject would achieve the inevitable profitable vocation, consequently this aspect at times has deterred the pathways chosen. Art was always the excelled subject and followed through for a lengthy period, however it had to be considered whether the future would lie in this area. A period of reflection followed during this time to lead to a decision, eventually it had to be decided that this was not where my preferred future would lie. Art however is a valuable skill to have and is reflected, if only faintly, within Marketing and Advertising BA honours.

Marketing and Advertising was, as it seemed at the time, a sum of all the favoured and achievable subjects to take. It was the obvious subject and one that has not been regretted. In fact it has surpassed my original expectations and continues to challenge and teach new things that are enormously interesting.

At present part time employment that has been taken has reflected these Marketing and Advertising studies. Working for a PR fulfilment company has brought an enlightening view into the world of Public Relations, even if it is only at the bottom and less attractive end of the 'job line'. It has given me networking opportunities and connections within the industry, and at present the opportunity to create and build relationships and work alongside people within an advertising career in mind. This could prove to be a reliable source in the future as well as an indication as to the career pathway to take within marketing and advertising.

Future Considerations

At present a decision has to be made, whether to choose a pathway into specialised marketing or advertising. This has proved to be an extremely difficult task. Does one choose something one prefers or something one will do well in? Reflecting upon Covey's original statement it would have to be said that the first should be the better option (the enjoyed preference). however it is still a hard decision to take. Another consideration is the one that is leading into the pathway that has already begun to be 'paved.'

The decision, at the moment all leads towards Advertising, however more research into each area will have to be taken before this becomes final. Where does one look to for this information and guidance? Talking to peers, lecturers, present and past students, reading the handbook for each pathway, instinct becomes more important. Nevertheless, is this enough?' Learning on the job' is where the decision lies, its context, surroundings and personal challenges will decide whether the job is where the career lies.

From a completely external point of view, the future on the whole lies within a career that keeps one challenged and entertained, one that allows individuals to climb the ladder and be proud of their individual achievements. One that is rewarding financially and mentally and one that satisfies. How much is this to ask, and how hard is this to achieve? The question that daunts thousands of people, is it realistic? Covey has some suggestions.

Currently, aspiration and belief in one self has got me this far, and a continued progress in this form of reflection will allow me to make many things achievable.

References
Chimaera Consulting Limited (1999) 'FAMOUS MODELS Covey's Habits' Chimaera (accessed 03.06.05) www.chimaeraconsulting.com/covey.htm

Colin Jones & Poems of Note

Bibliography

Mental Skills (2005) 'Communication Skills for Athletes: Feedback' Roy Robson (accessed: 03.06.05) www.mentalskills.co.uk/articles/featured_article.php?docid=10

Chimaera Consulting Limited (1999) 'FAMOUS MODELS Covey's Seven Habits' Chimaera (accessed: 03.06.05) http:///www.chimaeraconsulting.com/covey.htm

White Dove Books (2005) 'Stephen Covey's Principles of Effectiveness' Will Edwards (accessed: 03.06.05) http://www.whitedovebooks.co.uk/7-habits/7-habits.htm

LCC (2005) 'BAMA 2 Career Path Analysis – Managing Creativity and PPD' Lecture notes (accessed 10.03.05)

Luise Hales BAMA 2
PPD Assignment 2
Career path Analysis

Colin Jones & Poems of Note

Career Path Analysis

Joyce Saunders-Diop has been painting since the age of four, professionally since 1984 when she secured her first studio in London, but it's only when she began a freelance part-time career as a cell-painter in animation that her fine art career really gained momentum. S. Judd and P. Evans discovered similar patterns of foreseen and unforeseen work practices by art graduates (1999). The very controlled small scale and precise commercial artwork as well as its substantial and reliable financial rewards fuelled her expressionist and increasingly large-scale fine art work with the funds necessary for travel and numerous exhibitions, mainly in London, but also in Paris.

By 1996, the digital revolution had made cell-painters redundant and Joyce began a course of studies, which would lead her to the present day Masters Programme. Armed with an increasingly high level of computer graphic skills but also developing academic skills and knowledge on her second year of a BA (hons) in Digital Media Production at the then London College of Printing, she gradually found herself 'more self-directing and autonomous, more capable of controlling and directing responsibility for her learning and career projections', a consequence of 'reflective learning, critical reflection and self projection' (course notes, PPD 2002, Anthony Wailey). She read A. H. Maslow (1987) and discovered the concept of self-actualisation, which she still finds most interesting: 'Self-actualisation is intrinsic growth of what is already in the organism, or more accurately of what is the organism itself', 'to become everything that one is capable of becoming'. Studying colour, digital origination and graphic design draw on her affinities as an artist; finance and management lectures, projects and research enable her to sharpen an understanding of herself within the world of business. (Reflective diary, 2 December 2002).

She is re-evaluating her previous course of action as an artist and considering the best next avenues for maximum self-realisation.

Colin Jones & Poems of Note

Encouragingly, T. Putman (1999) describes the cultural, or creative industries as 'an area of above average growth', in Britain and J. Aston (1999) consolidates her belief that this course of studies is bound to enhance her future prospects.

At graduation level and beyond, Joyce hopes to have further developed into an individual as such but also within society at large who enjoys greater 'feelings of self-actualisation, self-fulfilment, self-realization of more and more complete development of fruition of (her) resources and potentialities and consequent feeling of growth, maturity, health and autonomy' (Maslow, 1997). With an understanding and application of the process by which concrete experience becomes reflective observation, conceptualisation and in turn active experimentation, (Kolb, 1984) she wants to have greater maturity, strength and control in the way she hopes to structure her future artistic projects.

These projects could be realised either in part-time or full-time self-employment as a painter, digital graphic-designer and /or muralist, set-designer, illustrator, computer animator or specialist techniques decorator. In order to support this portfolio career, she will probably revert to freelancing as a digital graphic designer or simply as a Photoshop, Illustrator and QuarkXpress Mac or PC operator. Subsequently, she could consider taking up a post as art director for a small to medium sized publication, if she feels confident in having acquired the relevant skills and knowledge and, probably most importantly, given the right contacts [see reference C. Eikeleberry PhD (1999)]. She hopes to have built a reasonably sound financial base within three years of starting her business and freelancing activities (2005 –2008) and to be able to work on increasingly challenging tasks.

A note on Sources

I will have acquired, while studying on this BA, enhanced cognitive skills and character traits such as those enumerated by A.H.Maslow (1997), for instance (pp43, 44):

Colin Jones & Poems of Note

Bibliography

-T. Jackson and E. Jackson (2001), The perfect CV, the Bath Press, Bath, GB.

-S. Jenner (2000), The graduate career handbook, Financial Times, Prentice Hall.

-I. Dumblow, H. Mac Lennan and N. Stanley (1999), Planning the future, NSEAD, Wiltshire.

-D. Leeds (1992), Marketing yourself, Judy Piatkus Publishers Ltd, London.

-A.H. Maslow (1987), Motivation and personality, Harper and Row Publishers Inc. , NY.

-C. Eikeleberry PhD (1999), The career guide for creative and unconventional people, revised, Ten Speed Press, Berkeley, Cal.

-Judith Humphries (1986), Kogan Page Ltd, London.

-R. N. Bolles (2000), What color is your parachute, Airlift books, UK.

Joyce Saunders Diop
BA Digital Media Production
PPD Assignment

Colin Jones & Poems of Note

Career Path Analysis

In 2000 Sarah-Jane Barclay completed her A-level examinations and left full time education to work for a construction company as an accounts administrator for one year. This was followed by 15 months spent travelling in Australia, New Zealand and Thailand. On her return she struggled with the direction she wanted to pursue for her career. A series of work placements in advertising agencies confirmed her belief that this was an area that interested her and so she applied for a BA Marketing and Advertising course at London College of Communication. Now at the end of the second year of her course and with further placements in advertising agencies, Sarah has decided that she would like to be an advertising copywriter in the future.

The decision process has proven difficult for the subject as she has had to work through each discipline meticulously disregarding one for another. She thought at first that her likely career would be as an account manager, however her experience working at Rainey Kelly Campbell Roafle Y&R advertising agency allowed her a good understanding of what is involved in running an advertising agency and what each person's role is within the company.

From this first hand experience Sarah was able to work through her options and choose the suitable career option from there. To be a copywriter is very difficult to break into. One needs to meet an art director they are comfortable working with and gain a lot of first hand experience working on live briefs before they can seek full time employment. To help Sarah achieve her goal she is aiming to gain a place at West Herts College on the Art Directing & Copywriting diploma course. This course is highly regarded by the creative industries and was recommended to Sarah whilst working in advertising agencies.

As part of the entry requirements for the course applicants must work on a set brief to qualify for an interview and have a portfolio of work to show. Working through some units of her degree course has allowed Sarah to begin to build her portfolio and gain experience working on briefs. The Managing Creativity unit set two briefs as assignments and this was a chance for Sarah to work creatively with a partner to practice her copywriting skills. She also enrolled on the copywriting skills Professional Development bolt-on course, which gave her more input into the discipline and also on a Photoshop skills course, a helpful programme on which to compose work.

With her future plans in mind Sarah needed to learn to balance her current work requirements for her degree course with the work needed for her future progression. The second year has proven challenging with large volumes of work including many group presentations which have taken up a lot of personal time and effort. By aiming for equilibrium between University work, copywriting work and personal time it was useful for the subject to look into the work of Stephen Covey and his Seven Habits of Highly Effective People.

Of the seven habits four were particularly useful; the notion of 'put first things first', 'win/win'. 'seek first to understand, then to be understood' and finally 'sharpen the saw' (Covey, 1989).

The concept of the time management matrix is very clear at pointing out the 'heart of personal management' (Covey, 1989). It is important to focus on achieving quadrant II activities by being proactive. The other skill learnt here is what it takes to say no.

'But you have to decide what your highest priorities are and have the courage – pleasantly, smiling, non apologetically – to say "no" to other things.'

Covey:156/7

These principles are important to take on board in order to balance a hectic and busy lifestyle with achieving all one's personal goals. This principle was found especially important for working in a group, and the attitude that it is not cruel to say no if it is not within the limits of one's capacity.

Also useful for working in a group is the 'win/win' principle.

'win/win is a belief in the third alternative. It's not your way or my way, it's a better way, a higher way.'

Covey: 207

To couple this theory with the abundance mentality, that 'there is plenty out there' for everybody, this model provides a positive way to look at work and also future goals.

With seeking first to understand then be understood, one looks at theory of 'selective listening versus empathic listening' (Covey, 1989). The notion that one should diagnose before they prescribe is a poignant statement when regarding working in a group. This is a useful skill to develop to aid both communication and relationships between not just colleagues but friends and family too.

Finally to 'sharpen the saw' demonstrates the 'Principles of Balanced Self-Renewal', (Covey:288)

PRINCIPLES OF BALANCED SELF-RENEWAL

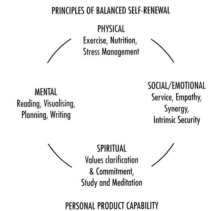

PHYSICAL
Exercise, Nutrition,
Stress Management

MENTAL
Reading, Visualising,
Planning, Writing

SOCIAL/EMOTIONAL
Service, Empathy,
Synergy,
Intrinsic Security

SPIRITUAL
Values clarification
& Commitment,
Study and Meditation

PERSONAL PRODUCT CAPABILITY

Colin Jones & Poems of Note

This is a good model to consider for balancing life and studies. Covey states that 'taking time to sharpen the saw is a definite quadrant II activity' (Covey: 289) which proves again how important time management is in living life 'effectively'. Ultimately organisation and planning is what Sarah must work on to achieve her goals and reach her full potential. By putting these theories into practice she will hopefully be able to work through her problems with less stress and difficulty. With her future plans ahead of her all she needs to concentrate on is to work hard in order to accomplish her ambitions.

References
Covey, S.R (1989), Seven habits of Highly Effective People, Simon & Schuster UK Ltd., London

Webography
http://www.businessballs.com/maslow.htm
http://www.businessballs.com/sevenhabitsstevencovey
http://www.belbin.info/
http://intranet.lcc.arts.ac.uk

Sarah Jane Barclay BAMA 2
PPD – Assignment 2

Contributor Biographies

I accepted the promise of the Holy Spirit and found my faith in God, through Jesus Christ during my first year at the University of the Arts London. From this point onwards I understood what life meant and became active in the UAL Christian Union where I made some good friends. I now work with a charity called Universities and Colleges Christian Fellowship (UCCF) in Southampton at Solent University. I am studying Christianity and the Arts and write and perform poetry in Church and at nightclubs. I still make books.

Ben Bell
BA Book Arts 2
School of Printing and Publishing

For the research and development of my major project I approached companies with my idea. This resulted in FHM endorsing my project and I now work for Clear Channel Outdoor designing dynamic presentations that are shown in over 50 countries. When I was first asked my opinion on an interactive piece of work at the company I answered that the professional, when delivering a presentation may not always want to have to cognitively think about where to click on the screen as they should be concentrating 100% on delivering a dynamic piece of work. The team agreed, so we adjusted the presentation accordingly. I believe that this was the first critical incident where I began a journey of self-belief in my own career.

Gary Brosnan
FDA Digital Media Production 2
School of Printing and Publishing

Having graduated into the big bad world with a Book Arts Degree, I am looking for an agent to represent me and promote my work on children's books. Trying to avoid selling my soul to the devil to pay the bills means a tragic menial job while I chase my dream but the writing and illustration does provide me with an excuse to come home, drink Rosie Lee, and creatively 'vent' at the end of a long hard day. In the meantime I am exhibiting various illustrations and paintings in a French gallery and restaurant, which I hope will at least earn me enough money for a pair of sexy new shoes. I am hoping to become successful enough to work with writing and illustration on a full time basis.

Nicola Carey
BA Book Arts 2
School of Printing and Publishing

Shantelle Carty successfully balanced her studies with looking after her young son. She now works part time at the Home Office in Croydon. She is looking for a job in Marketing but so far has been unsuccessful and is trying all her options, seeking careers advice. Shantelle's son recently started school. He was very excited and is doing really well, Shantelle is very proud of him.

Shantelle Carty
HND Retail Management
The Marketing School

Through taking FDA Digital Media Production I realised that a multi-media course is not for me so I decided to pursue my interest in Graphic Design, visual merchandising and point-of-sale. I have become more interested in the area of bringing the promotion of a product into a consumer environment. I plan to take an evening class in graphic design at LCC.

Graham Crew
FDA Digital Media Production 2
School of Printing and Publishing

I greatly underestimated life after studying, I especially remember lecturers saying; "these are the best days of your life". Finding work is the most stressful thing I have ever incurred. Doors do open if you keep knocking hard enough. My faith in God has helped me along the way and taught me to be thankful for every situation that I am in because there is always a lesson to be learnt. I am currently working part time for my local council, I occasionally write poetry, it was a huge part of my life at one stage and I would like to go back to this, my first love, but at this moment in time I want to concentrate on other areas in my life.

Lynette Dias
BA Marketing and Advertising 2
The Marketing School

I studied Marketing and Advertising due to my interest in the subject and for the skills I would learn to help market myself in my dream career. My ambition is to become a professional singer-songwriter and in between studies I have always juggled singing, writing, recording and performing. Since leaving university I have been working hard on pursuing my music and am currently recording my debut album. I am also training to be a life coach and am hoping to combine the two areas to help make positive changes in the people I encounter and (as corny as it might sound) help them to spread the love too...as Tony Robbins says, "Pass on the contribution" Keep up to date by visiting my website www. kellyerez.com

Kelly Erez
BA Marketing and Advertising 2
The Marketing School

I am currently seeking employment in the graphic design world. In the last six years I have struggled to juggle a hectic life style and study and finally I made it. Straight after University I went on a well earned holiday for a month to Iraq where I did a lot of soul searching and came back knowing that I wanted to find my place in the design world. I love writing, so maybe one day in the right place in my life I may fulfil my dream of writing a book. Who knows what the future may hold, but for now I am awaiting my destiny. The real world is harder than I thought but I'm doing the best I can with what I have.

Kanda Faraj
FDA Design for Graphic Communication 2
School of Graphic Design

After completing my degree I went travelling around Europe, ending up in my parent's birthplace, St. Lucia. After graduation I started the rigorous task of finding a full time job where I could put what I had learnt from my degree to good use. I am currently working for Ladbrokes doing a couple of days a week, while working for various agencies, filling marketing and administrative positions. I enjoy putting theory into practice by promoting small local businesses. I intend to continue travelling and to hopefully end up in Canada as I have been looking for jobs on a global scale and Canada seems to have great prospects. In the near future I will take a short course in Events Management.

Charlene James
BA Marketing and Advertising 2
The Marketing School

After graduating Maria went to the city of Angels for two months and worked for ZinaVasi who specialise in linen. The job involved photographing/preparing the stock for print for clients such as Bloomingdales and Bed Bath and Beyond. She then went back to London and worked as a dresser at London Fashion Week. At the moment Maria is Freelancing/Collaborating with various artists producing work such as fliers for the Lincoln Lounge and two installations in the Regent Street and Oxford Street OASIS stores. Possible collaborations with Favela Chic may happen in the near future.

Maria Karpouchina
BA Graphics and Media Design 2
School of Graphic Design

After working with different media at LCC I chose Information Design. I now work as a freelancer designing product packaging, seeing products through to completion. I have been in Jeddah, Saudi Arabia, where I have been involved in a number of projects. I taught children how to draw portraits and caricatures at Continental School and worked with Deep Agency, a design agency creating illustrations for children's books and designing a brochure for Crystal Beach resort. I have also been designing a Brand for a new cancer charity organization, spreading awareness through design material. I wish to further my creativity in different design fields such as web development and moving image. In three years from now I plan to open my own design agency in London.

Tuline Malecki
FDA Graphic Design 2
School of Graphic Design

After Graduating I felt relieved that the exams, dissertations and essays were all over. I thoroughly enjoyed my time at University I got a 2.1 which I really wasn't expecting as I am not the cleverest bean. I temped while waiting to hear from prospective employers, trying every possible means. I now work at the Barking & Dagenham Chamber of Commerce part time as a Marketing & Recruitment Officer and also work as a Clinique Consultant. I am ultimately working towards having my own business organisation, perhaps a Marketing Consultancy for Business Organisations just starting up.

Dawn Mansell
BA Marketing and Advertising 2
The Marketing School

I graduated in 2005 with a first class Honours degree in Information Design after completing my FDA at LCC. I have been freelancing ever since. I am looking for full-time work and have also enrolled onto a self-study course run by Skills Train to learn web design. I'm now 24 and getting grey hairs trying to figure out where to go next in life. But I now have a bit of fame at last, with this publication even though it is not in my field of work.

Sue Phan Tue
FDA Design for Graphic Communication 2
School of Graphic Design

For me college ended at the handing-in date, it was on that day that I realised I would have to function on my own in future. The last event that involved all of my class was the final show "Not all those who wonder are lost" www.thosewhowonder.com I then undertook an internship with "Staempfli", a big media and publishing house in Switzerland. This job made me determined to work for myself. Equipped with lots of prepress and print knowledge I came back to London and worked for "Onedotzero" an animation production company also managing a lot of events and screenings worldwide. I have founded a limited company called "dandelion & burdock" with a fellow graduate of LCC. (www.dandelion-burdock.com) We offer illustration, graphic design and moving image to our clients.

Nils Porrman
BA Graphics and Media Design 2
School of Graphic Design

After a break away from studying, Matt Ringsell is now in the final year of a BA in Digital Media Production at LCC. He specialises in video, music and CD-Rom production, photography, and digital imaging. He plays bass and provides backing vocals in 'Highrise,' an indie-punk rock band from North London who played 20 gigs in the capital in the year 2005. Until recently he ran a successful club night in Chalk Farm called 'Shock 'n' Awe Tactic,' He currently works part time as a Production Manager for the award winning photographers, Hyatt Studios in Tring, Hertfordshire.

Matt Ringsell
FDA Digital Media Production 2
School of Printing and Publishing

Since the age of four Joyce Jocelyne Saunders- Diop has been a practicing artist. Using a variety of media and stylistic approaches Joyce produces work ranging from small illustrations for newspapers to large paintings that cover three story building façades. Her work has been exhibited in London and Paris since 1984. Since recently graduating , she promotes her business at LCC on the MA in Enterprise and Management for the Creative Arts and continues to exhibit on a regular basis.

Joyce Saunders-Diop
BA Digital Media Production 3
School of Printing and Publishing

Dan Simpson is currently in his second year of a three-year Media Practice and Theory degree at the University of Sussex. As well as his University studies he also works on various projects including producing and directing promotional videos, filming and editing theatre pieces at the Theatre Royal Brighton, organising a Film Festival and watching his beloved Sheffield United.

Dan Simpson
Foundation Media
School of Media

After graduating I went straight to working fulltime with my husband running a company that makes architectural models. My role is split between being a Creative Director and a freelance Architectural Photographer. Six months after graduating I discovered I had cancer, I had a mastectomy, 5 months of chemotherapy and 3 weeks of radiotherapy. This will be followed by 5 years of drug therapy and however awful it has been I must say it has probably been the most positive experience I have ever had.

I continue with my professional work. We regularly exhibit at the Royal Academy Summer Exhibition and the Venice Architectural Biennale. I co-designed a large exhibition for Urban Living in Manchester based on the concept of Super cities developed by architect Will Alsop.

Sally Spencer-Davies
BA Digital Media Production 3
School of Printing and Publishing

Colin Jones & Poems of Note

I went straight from University to working as a freelancer on a research project for a British Furniture Designer. I repositioned his brand by focusing on communications within his existing stores and future company plans and then created a new look and a monthly newsletter. The business has increased its orders by 20% since the project. I then went into the wonderful world of the fashion industry working as an agent for a Danish label that has been the top brand in Denmark for three years in a row. Whatever the future holds for me, I hope it involves becoming rich so I can concentrate on my real passion, writing. University for me brought together a group of girls who have changed my life forever.

Kim Viner
BA Marketing and Advertising 2
The Marketing School

Colin Jones & Poems of Note

LCC Staff Contributors

Carlton Boulter, School of Media

Jason Copley, School of Media

Graham Goldwater, School of Graphic Design

Kathy Hilton, School of Media

Julie James, The Marketing School

Catherine Johnson, Royal Literary Fund

John Mcarthy, School of Media

Gary Naylor, School of Media

Andy Savery, Quality and Marketing Unit

Lily Sawyer School of Media

Catherine Smith, School of Graphic Design

John Stephens, School of Printing and Publishing

Heather Symonds, Quality and Marketing Unit

Sarah Temple, School of Graphic Design

Tony Wailey, Quality and Marketing Unit

Julia Yates, Creative Careers Service